Gecko

by Jessica Rudolph

Consultant: Thane Maynard, Director
Cincinnati Zoo and Botanical Garden
Cincinnati, Ohio

BEARPORT
PUBLISHING

New York, New York

Credits

Cover, © Ale-ks/Deposit Photos; TOC, © Worraket/Shutterstock; 4–5, © Blickwinkel/Alamy; 6, © S. Blair Hedges/epa/Corbis; 7, © Milan Kořínek; 8T, © reptiles4all/Shutterstock; 8M, © Kefca/Shutterstock; 8B, © tarikh/iStock; 9, © Dobermaraner/Shutterstock; 10L, © po808/fotolia; 10R, © tanoochai/Shutterstock; 11, © Mgkuijpers/Dreamstime; 12, © Hotshotsworldwide/Dreamstime; 13, © CathyKeifer/iStock; 14, © iSiripong/Shutterstock; 15, © Damian Ryszawy/Shutterstock; 16, © Zybilo/Dreamstime; 17, © Chutima Chaochaiya/Shutterstock; 18–19, © AaronPattison/iStock; 20–21, © Cathy Keifer/Shutterstock; 22T, © Cathy Keifer/Shutterstock; 22M, © Flirt/Alamy; 22B, © Matt Jeppson/Shutterstock; 23TL, © Pavel Vakhrushev/Shutterstock; 23TR, © encikAn/Shutterstock; 23BL, © FlavoredPixels/Shutterstock; 23BR, © Mario Madrona Barrera/Dreamstime.

Publisher: Kenn Goin
Editor: J. Clark
Creative Director: Spencer Brinker
Design: Debrah Kaiser
Photo Researcher: Olympia Shannon

Library of Congress Cataloging-in-Publication Data

Rudolph, Jessica, author.
  Gecko / by Jessica Rudolph.
    pages cm. — (Weird But cute)
  Includes bibliographical references and index.
  ISBN 978-1-62724-849-5 (library binding) — ISBN 1-62724-849-8 (library binding)
  1. Geckos—Juvenile literature. I. Title.
  QL666.L245R83 2016
  597.95'2—dc23
                                    2015008807

For more information, write to Bearport Publishing Company, Inc., 45 West 21st Street, Suite 3B, New York, New York 10010. Printed in the United States of America.

10 9 8 7 6 5 4 3 2 1

Contents

What's this weird but cute **lizard**?

Big **eye**s!

It's a gecko.

Colorful, bumpy skin!

Strange toes!

5

Geckos live all over the world.

They live in forests, deserts, and on mountains.

giant gecko

dwarf gecko

giant gecko

Yellow, blue, red, green, orange.

Many geckos are very colorful.

Some have stripes or spots.

leopard gecko

9

Geckos can climb straight up trees.

They can hang upside down on rocks, too.

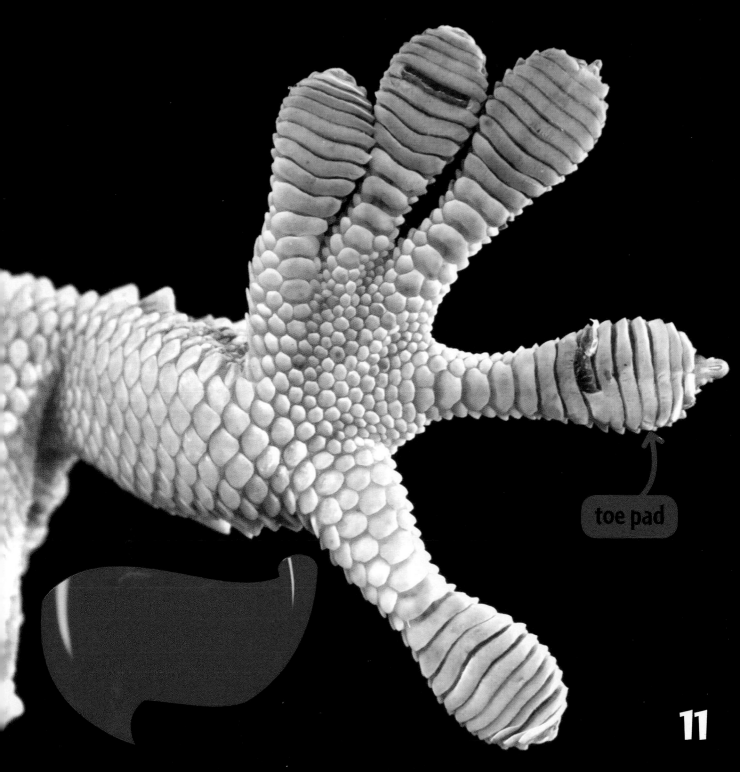

toe pad

11

On the hunt!

Geckos climb everywhere to look for food.

The little lizards eat worms, **insects**, and fruit.

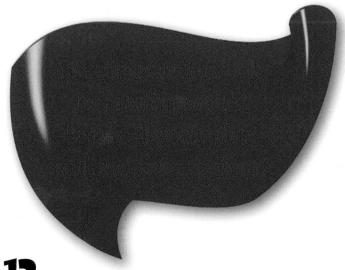

dragonfly

cricket

Where did the lizard go?

a gecko that looks like a dead leaf

14

Some geckos blend in with leaves or tree **bark**.

This helps them hide from enemies.

If an enemy grabs a gecko's tail, the tail will break off.

Then the gecko can run away.

new tail

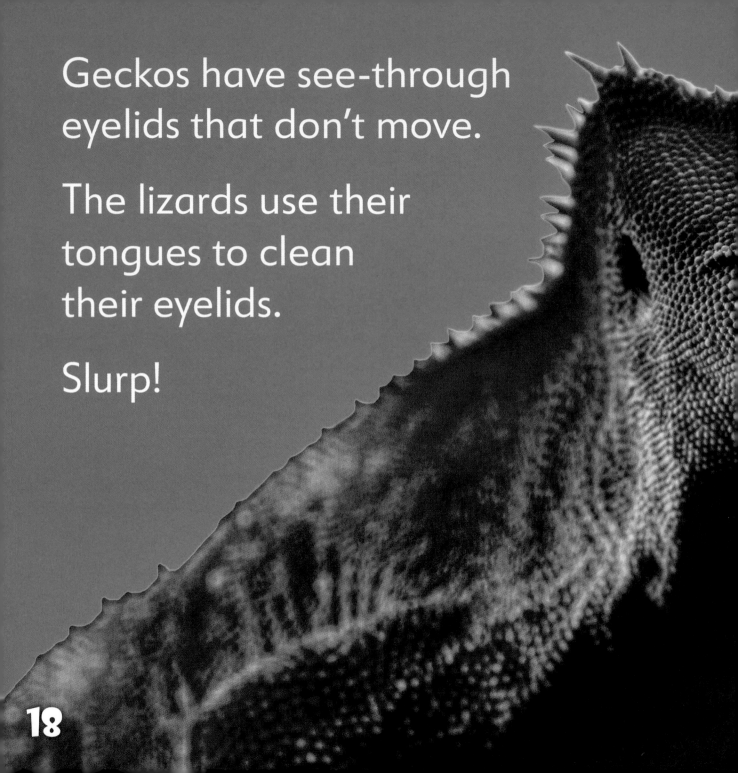

Geckos have see-through eyelids that don't move.

The lizards use their tongues to clean their eyelids.

Slurp!

eyelid

Chirp!
Bark!
Click!

Geckos make
lots of noises.

More Weird Lizards

Chameleon
This lizard has a very long, sticky tongue. It stretches out its tongue to catch insects.

Collared Lizard
The collared lizard eats insects, spiders, and other lizards. When it runs after an animal, the collared lizard can rise up on its two back legs!

Horned Lizard
The horned lizard has spikes all over its body. The spikes help prevent enemies such as hawks from eating the lizard.

Glossary

bark (BARK) the tough covering on a tree

insects (IN-sekts) small animals that have six legs, two antennae, three main body parts, and a hard covering called an exoskeleton

lizard (LIZ-urd) a reptile that has a scaly body and, usually, four legs and a long tail

toe pads (TOH PADZ) round, sticky parts at the ends of a gecko's feet

Index

Read More

Connors, Kathleen. *Geckos (Really Wild Reptiles).* New York: Gareth Stevens (2013).

Velthaus, Sally. *Geckos (World of Reptiles).* Mankato, MN: Capstone (2006).

Learn More Online

To learn more about geckos, visit
www.bearportpublishing.com/WeirdButCute

About the Author

Jessica Rudolph lives in Connecticut. She has edited and written many books about history, science, and nature for children.